PRINCEWILL LAGANG

Cultivating Trust and Security

First published by PRINCEWILL LAGANG 2023

Copyright © 2023 by Princewill Lagang

All rights reserved. No part of this publication may be reproduced, stored or transmitted in any form or by any means, electronic, mechanical, photocopying, recording, scanning, or otherwise without written permission from the publisher. It is illegal to copy this book, post it to a website, or distribute it by any other means without permission.

Princewill Lagang asserts the moral right to be identified as the author of this work.

First edition

This book was professionally typeset on Reedsy.
Find out more at reedsy.com

Contents

1	Introduction to Cultivating Trust and Security	1
2	Understanding the Elements of Trust	4
3	Building Blocks of Security in Relationships	7
4	Communication and Transparency	10
5	Reliability and Consistency	14
6	Navigating Challenges and Conflict Together	17
7	Emotional Availability and Vulnerability	20
8	Rebuilding Trust After Betrayal	23
9	Trusting Yourself and Your Partner	26
10	Fostering Mutual Respect and Support	29
11	Encouraging Personal Growth and Autonomy	32
12	The Ongoing Journey of Cultivating Trust and Security	35

1

Introduction to Cultivating Trust and Security

In a world that thrives on connections and interactions, the concepts of trust and security hold unparalleled significance. At the heart of every relationship—be it personal, professional, or societal—lies the fundamental need for trust and security. In this opening chapter, we delve into the multifaceted importance of these intertwined concepts, setting the stage for an exploration of strategies aimed at fortifying these essential foundations.

Defining the Importance of Trust and Security in Relationships

Trust, often described as the cornerstone of any healthy relationship, serves as the adhesive that binds individuals together. It is the confidence we place in others' intentions, actions, and words. Trust fosters vulnerability, allowing individuals to open themselves to each other, share their thoughts, feelings, and ideas, and collaborate effectively. Without trust, relationships stagnate, communication breaks down, and conflicts escalate.

Security, on the other hand, is the protective shield that assures individuals of their well-being within a relationship. It encompasses emotional, physical, and psychological safety. When people feel secure, they can freely express themselves, take risks, and engage in honest conversations. Security acts as the stable foundation upon which trust can flourish.

The importance of trust and security extends beyond interpersonal relationships. In the realm of businesses and organizations, trust plays a pivotal role in employee engagement, customer loyalty, and successful partnerships. Similarly, in the digital age, cybersecurity has become paramount as individuals and societies rely heavily on technology for communication, financial transactions, and more. Without a sense of security, these interactions become laden with risk and suspicion.

Setting the Stage for Exploring Strategies to Strengthen These Foundations

As we embark on a journey to understand and cultivate trust and security, it is imperative to recognize that building and maintaining these foundations require intentional effort. Just as a garden needs constant tending to flourish, relationships demand continuous nurturing to thrive.

Throughout this book, we will navigate a spectrum of strategies that empower individuals to foster trust and security. We will explore effective communication techniques that promote transparency and authenticity. We will delve into the psychology of trust, unraveling the factors that contribute to its formation and the reasons behind its erosion. Examining real-life case studies and examples, we will uncover the consequences of breached trust and compromised security.

Moreover, we will delve into the delicate balance between trust and vulnerability. We'll discuss how embracing vulnerability can lead to stronger connections, and how establishing boundaries contributes to a sense of security. The digital landscape will not be overlooked, as we delve into ways to bolster cybersecurity and protect sensitive information in an increasingly interconnected world.

In conclusion, this chapter serves as a prelude to our exploration of trust and security. By understanding their significance and the far-reaching impact they hold, we set the groundwork for an insightful journey. As we delve into the subsequent chapters, we will equip ourselves with tools, knowledge, and strategies to cultivate trust and security in a variety of contexts, ultimately enriching our relationships and enhancing our interactions.

2

Understanding the Elements of Trust

Trust is a multifaceted concept that forms the bedrock of healthy relationships. In this chapter, we delve deeper into the elements that contribute to the construction of trust, examining how they interact within the intricate web of human connections.

Identifying the Key Components that Contribute to Building Trust

Trust is not a monolithic entity; it is composed of various interconnected components that combine to form a holistic sense of reliability. These components include:

1. Reliability: The consistent ability of an individual to fulfill their commitments and promises. Reliability establishes predictability in relationships, fostering a sense of assurance.

2. Honesty: The practice of truthfulness and transparency. Honesty builds a foundation of open communication, encouraging individuals to share their thoughts and feelings without fear of manipulation.

3. Integrity: The alignment of actions with values and principles. Integrity reflects an individual's ethical stance and consistency in behavior, enhancing credibility.

4. Benevolence: Demonstrating goodwill and genuine concern for others' well-being. Acts of benevolence underscore intentions that extend beyond self-interest, reinforcing trustworthiness.

5. Competence: Displaying the necessary skills, knowledge, and abilities to fulfill responsibilities. Competence instills confidence in an individual's capability to deliver on their commitments.

Exploring the Dynamics of Trust within the Context of Relationships

Trust is not static; it evolves over time based on interactions and experiences. The dynamics of trust within relationships are influenced by various factors:

1. Initial Impressions: First impressions can set the tone for trust-building. Positive initial interactions lay the groundwork for future rapport, while negative experiences can hinder the development of trust.

2. Consistency: Consistent behavior over time reinforces trust. Individuals who uphold their promises and demonstrate reliability are more likely to be perceived as trustworthy.

3. Vulnerability: Sharing vulnerabilities and personal stories can deepen connections and build trust. When individuals reveal their authentic selves, it encourages reciprocity and openness.

4. Communication: Open and transparent communication is crucial for trust. Miscommunication, secrecy, or withholding information can erode trust and lead to misunderstandings.

5. Conflict Resolution: How conflicts are handled can impact trust. Resolving disagreements respectfully and constructively can strengthen trust by demonstrating a commitment to the relationship's well-being.

6. Recovery from Betrayal: Trust can be shattered by betrayal. The process of rebuilding trust after a breach involves acknowledging the betrayal, expressing remorse, and consistent efforts to regain trust.

7. Shared Experiences: Engaging in shared experiences and overcoming challenges together fosters a sense of unity and camaraderie, which can enhance trust.

As we navigate the intricate dance of trust within relationships, it is essential to recognize that trust-building is a continuous process. Just as a fragile seed grows into a sturdy tree through nurturing and care, trust flourishes when nurtured through positive interactions and genuine efforts.

In the subsequent chapters, we will delve into practical strategies that leverage these components and dynamics to foster trust and fortify relationships. Through introspection, understanding, and intentional actions, we can navigate the delicate terrain of trust-building, enriching our connections with others.

3

Building Blocks of Security in Relationships

Security forms the foundation upon which trust can thrive, creating an environment in which individuals feel safe, valued, and empowered. This chapter delves into the essential components that contribute to emotional safety and security within relationships, along with strategies for cultivating this vital bedrock.

The Role of Emotional Safety and Security in Fostering a Healthy Connection

Emotional safety and security are paramount for establishing a healthy and thriving connection between individuals. When individuals feel emotionally secure, they are more likely to express their authentic selves, share their innermost thoughts and feelings, and engage in open and honest communication. This safety net allows for vulnerability, which in turn deepens intimacy and understanding.

Emotional safety encompasses:

CULTIVATING TRUST AND SECURITY

1. Non-judgment: Creating an environment where individuals can freely express themselves without fear of criticism or judgment.

2. Validation: Acknowledging and affirming each other's emotions and experiences, ensuring that feelings are respected and understood.

3. Empathy: Cultivating an empathetic understanding of each other's perspectives, fostering a sense of mutual support and compassion.

4. Consistency: Maintaining a consistent presence and emotional availability, which builds a sense of stability and predictability.

5. Respect for Boundaries: Honoring each other's boundaries and preferences, creating an atmosphere of respect and autonomy.

Strategies for Creating a Secure Environment for Both Partners

1. Active Listening: Engage in active listening, providing your partner with your full attention and showing genuine interest in their thoughts and feelings. This encourages open dialogue and demonstrates respect.

2. Open Communication: Foster an environment where both partners feel comfortable discussing their needs, concerns, and aspirations. Encourage honest conversations and be receptive to feedback.

3. Affection and Reassurance: Regularly express affection and provide reassurance to your partner. Small gestures, affirmations, and physical touch can reinforce feelings of security.

4. Conflict Resolution Skills: Develop healthy conflict resolution skills that emphasize collaboration and compromise rather than hostility. Address conflicts with empathy and the intention of finding common ground.

5. Shared Goals and Values: Establish shared goals and values that create a sense of unity. Aligning your aspirations strengthens the foundation of the relationship.

6. Quality Time: Dedicate quality time to nurturing the relationship. Engage in activities that promote connection and shared experiences.

7. Consistency and Reliability: Uphold your commitments and be consistent in your actions. Reliability builds trust and reinforces the sense of security.

8. Acknowledging and Honoring Emotions: Create an environment where emotions are acknowledged and respected. Avoid belittling or dismissing feelings.

9. Respect for Autonomy: Recognize and honor each other's independence. Encourage personal growth and maintain a sense of self while fostering togetherness.

10. Reassuring Gestures: Engage in gestures that offer reassurance, such as a supportive touch during difficult times or a simple "I'm here for you" message.

In nurturing emotional safety and security, it's important to remember that every relationship is unique. Understanding your partner's needs and preferences is key to tailoring these strategies to your specific dynamic. By creating a secure and nurturing environment, you pave the way for trust to flourish and the relationship to thrive.

4

Communication and Transparency

Open and honest communication serves as the lifeblood of trust-building within relationships. In this chapter, we delve into the pivotal role that effective communication plays in nurturing trust, and explore various techniques for fostering transparency and maintaining clear dialogue.

The Pivotal Role of Open and Honest Communication in Trust-Building

Communication acts as the bridge connecting individuals' thoughts, emotions, and intentions. It is through communication that trust is nurtured, as it allows individuals to express themselves authentically, share vulnerabilities, and align expectations. Open and honest communication breeds understanding, minimizes misunderstandings, and reinforces the sense of emotional safety.

Effective communication:

1. Fosters Understanding: Clear and thoughtful communication promotes mutual understanding, reducing the likelihood of misinterpretation and

conflict.

2. Encourages Vulnerability: Transparent communication encourages individuals to share their thoughts, fears, and aspirations, deepening connections and fostering trust.

3. Builds Rapport: Frequent and genuine communication creates rapport and intimacy, establishing a foundation of reliability and authenticity.

4. Addresses Issues: Effective communication allows problems to be addressed openly, preventing them from escalating into larger issues that erode trust.

5. Promotes Emotional Safety: A safe space for communication nurtures emotional safety, enabling individuals to express themselves without fear of judgment or rejection.

Techniques for Fostering Transparency and Maintaining Clear Dialogue

1. Active Listening: Give your full attention when your partner speaks. Listen not just to the words, but also to the emotions and nuances behind them.

2. I-Statements: Use "I" statements to express your feelings and thoughts. This approach avoids blame and fosters ownership of emotions.

3. Empathetic Responses: Respond with empathy to show understanding and validation. Reflect back what your partner is saying to demonstrate that you're truly engaged.

4. Non-Verbal Communication: Pay attention to non-verbal cues like body language and facial expressions. They often reveal emotions that words may not express.

5. Scheduled Conversations: Designate regular times for conversations about important topics. This prevents issues from being brushed aside and ensures they are addressed.

6. Clear Expression of Expectations: Discuss your expectations openly and honestly. Clarify what each partner wants from the relationship to avoid misunderstandings.

7. Regular Check-Ins: Have periodic check-ins to discuss how the relationship is progressing. Address concerns and celebrate achievements together.

8. Conflict Resolution Strategies: Learn and implement effective conflict resolution techniques. Focus on understanding the issue, finding common ground, and working together to find solutions.

9. Sharing Thoughts and Feelings: Be willing to share your thoughts, even if they are difficult or uncomfortable. Vulnerability promotes trust and understanding.

10. Acknowledging Mistakes: Own up to your mistakes and apologize when necessary. This shows accountability and reinforces trust through honesty.

11. Avoid Assumptions: Clarify any assumptions or interpretations before jumping to conclusions. Misunderstandings can be avoided by seeking clarification.

12. Feedback Loops: Create an environment where giving and receiving feedback is encouraged. Constructive feedback helps partners grow together.

By consistently practicing open and transparent communication, partners lay the foundation for a relationship built on trust. Through understanding, empathy, and shared dialogue, they create an environment where authenticity and vulnerability flourish, deepening their connection and strengthening their emotional bond.

5

Reliability and Consistency

Reliability and consistency are the bedrock upon which trust and security are built within relationships. In this chapter, we explore the profound impact that being dependable and consistent has on fostering trust, and delve into strategies for upholding commitments and promises.

How Reliability and Consistency Contribute to Trust and Security

Reliability and consistency are the threads that weave together the fabric of trust. When individuals consistently follow through on their commitments and promises, it establishes a track record of dependability. This predictability fosters a sense of security, assuring others that they can count on their partner's actions matching their words. Reliability and consistency create a stable environment where individuals feel valued, respected, and safe.

Key contributions of reliability and consistency:

1. Predictability: Consistent behavior creates predictability, reducing uncertainty and anxiety within the relationship.

RELIABILITY AND CONSISTENCY

2. Trust Reinforcement: Demonstrating reliability over time reinforces trust, showing that intentions are aligned with actions.

3. Emotional Safety: Dependability cultivates emotional safety, as individuals know they can rely on their partner during both good times and challenges.

4. Conflict Mitigation: In times of conflict, past reliability serves as a foundation for resolution. Partners are more likely to believe that issues will be addressed constructively.

5. Authenticity: Consistency showcases an individual's authenticity, ensuring that they don't change their behavior based on circumstances.

Strategies for Following Through on Commitments and Promises

1. Realistic Goal-Setting: Set achievable goals and make commitments that you can realistically fulfill. Avoid overcommitting and prioritize quality over quantity.

2. Clear Communication: Clearly communicate your intentions, timelines, and limitations. Be transparent about what you can and cannot do.

3. Prioritization: Prioritize commitments based on their importance and urgency. This helps prevent overwhelming situations and ensures that essential tasks are completed.

4. Use of Calendar and Reminders: Utilize calendars, planners, and reminders to keep track of commitments and deadlines. Technology can be a valuable tool for staying organized.

5. Accountability Partners: Share your commitments with a trusted friend or partner who can help keep you accountable.

6. Break Down Tasks: Divide larger commitments into smaller, manageable tasks. This prevents feeling overwhelmed and increases the likelihood of follow-through.

7. Honesty About Limitations: Be honest about your limitations. If circumstances change, communicate this promptly and offer alternatives.

8. Review and Reflect: Regularly review your commitments and assess your progress. Reflect on what you've learned and adjust your approach if needed.

9. Learn to Say No: Be selective about new commitments. Learn to decline when you're already stretched thin to avoid overextending yourself.

10. Apologize and Amend: If you're unable to meet a commitment, apologize sincerely and communicate your revised plan to make amends.

11. Celebrate Achievements: Celebrate the successful completion of commitments, whether big or small. This positive reinforcement encourages continued reliability.

By practicing reliability and consistency, individuals create an environment of trust that allows relationships to flourish. Demonstrating that one's words align with actions builds a sense of security that strengthens connections and fosters a lasting bond.

6

Navigating Challenges and Conflict Together

Challenges and conflicts are inevitable aspects of any relationship, but they can also serve as opportunities to enhance trust and deepen connections. In this chapter, we explore the transformative power of addressing conflicts as avenues for trust-building. We also delve into techniques that allow partners to resolve disagreements while preserving trust and strengthening their bond.

Addressing Conflicts as Opportunities to Enhance Trust

Contrary to popular belief, conflicts are not necessarily detrimental to relationships. When navigated effectively, conflicts can become catalysts for growth, understanding, and trust-building. Viewing conflicts as opportunities allows partners to engage in open dialogue, share perspectives, and work together to find solutions. Addressing conflicts head-on demonstrates a commitment to the relationship's well-being and reinforces the foundation of trust.

Benefits of addressing conflicts as opportunities:

1. Heightened Understanding: Conflicts often stem from differing perspectives. Addressing them fosters understanding of each other's viewpoints, leading to increased empathy and connection.

2. Improved Communication: Conflict resolution requires effective communication. Partners learn to express themselves clearly and listen actively, enhancing overall communication skills.

3. Problem-Solving Skills: Resolving conflicts builds problem-solving skills. Partners learn to collaborate and find mutually acceptable solutions.

4. Trust Reinforcement: Successfully navigating conflicts reinforces trust. When partners work together to resolve issues, it demonstrates their commitment to the relationship's success.

5. Emotional Connection: Engaging in open and respectful conflict resolution deepens the emotional connection between partners.

Techniques for Resolving Disagreements While Preserving Trust

1. Stay Calm: Approach conflicts with a calm and composed demeanor. Emotional reactions can escalate tensions and hinder productive dialogue.

2. Active Listening: Listen actively and attentively to your partner's perspective. Show empathy and reflect their feelings to ensure they feel heard.

3. Express Feelings: Use "I" statements to express your feelings and thoughts. Avoid blame and focus on your emotions and needs.

4. Avoid Blame: Focus on the issue at hand rather than assigning blame. Use

collaborative language that promotes working together to find solutions.

5. Take Breaks: If emotions escalate, take a break to cool down. Return to the conversation with a clearer mindset.

6. Identify Underlying Needs: Dig deeper to uncover underlying needs or concerns that might be contributing to the conflict.

7. Find Common Ground: Identify areas of agreement and build on those as you work toward a solution.

8. Brainstorm Solutions: Collaboratively brainstorm potential solutions that address both partners' needs.

9. Compromise: Be willing to compromise and find middle ground. Remember that no one solution will satisfy both parties completely.

10. Learn from Conflicts: After resolution, reflect on what was learned from the conflict. Discuss ways to prevent similar issues in the future.

11. Appreciate Efforts: Express appreciation for your partner's willingness to address conflicts and work toward resolutions.

12. Professional Help: If conflicts persist or escalate, consider seeking the guidance of a professional therapist or counselor.

By approaching conflicts as opportunities to strengthen trust, partners can transform potentially damaging situations into moments of growth and connection. Through respectful communication, active listening, and a commitment to finding common ground, conflicts can become stepping stones towards deeper understanding and a stronger bond.

7

Emotional Availability and Vulnerability

Emotional availability and vulnerability are powerful conduits through which trust is nurtured and deepened within relationships. In this chapter, we delve into the profound connection between emotional openness and trust-building. We also explore strategies for cultivating vulnerability and fostering emotional bonds that contribute to a strong foundation of trust.

Exploring the Connection between Emotional Openness and Trust

Emotional availability involves being present and receptive to your own emotions as well as your partner's feelings. Vulnerability, on the other hand, requires courageously sharing your innermost thoughts, fears, and insecurities. Both emotional availability and vulnerability are essential for trust-building, as they create an atmosphere of authenticity and empathy. When individuals openly express their emotions and are receptive to their partner's feelings, they create a space where trust can flourish.

The connection between emotional openness and trust:

1. Authenticity: Sharing genuine emotions fosters authenticity, which is fundamental for building trust. Authenticity assures partners that each person's intentions are sincere.

2. Empathy: Emotional availability encourages partners to empathize with each other's experiences and emotions, deepening their understanding of one another.

3. Connection: Vulnerability creates a unique connection by allowing partners to share their inner worlds. This connection strengthens the emotional bond and reinforces trust.

4. Mutual Support: When partners are emotionally available, they can provide support and comfort during challenging times, reinforcing the sense of security.

5. Positive Feedback Loop: Emotional openness and vulnerability lead to positive feedback, as partners reciprocate by sharing their own feelings. This creates a cycle of deeper connection.

Strategies for Cultivating Vulnerability and Deepening Emotional Bonds

1. Self-Awareness: Cultivate self-awareness to understand your own emotions and needs. This self-awareness forms the foundation for open communication.

2. Create a Safe Space: Establish an environment where both partners feel safe to share their thoughts and feelings without fear of judgment.

3. Start Small: Begin by sharing minor feelings or experiences before delving into deeper emotions. Gradually build up to more vulnerable topics.

4. Lead by Example: Be willing to be vulnerable yourself. Sharing your own

feelings encourages your partner to reciprocate.

5. Active Listening: Create opportunities for your partner to share without interruption. Be an attentive and empathetic listener.

6. Ask Open-Ended Questions: Encourage open dialogue by asking questions that require more than a simple yes or no answer. This invites deeper sharing.

7. Express Empathy: Show understanding and empathy when your partner shares their feelings. Validate their emotions without judgment.

8. Normalize Vulnerability: Discuss the importance of vulnerability and emotional openness within the relationship. Normalize the act of sharing feelings.

9. Avoid Criticism: When your partner shares their vulnerabilities, avoid criticizing or dismissing their feelings. Create a judgment-free zone.

10. Celebrate Shared Experiences: Engage in activities that encourage vulnerability, such as discussing personal goals or dreams, to foster emotional connection.

11. Express Gratitude: Express appreciation for your partner's willingness to share their feelings. This reinforces the value of vulnerability.

12. Practice Patience: Building emotional bonds and vulnerability takes time. Be patient and allow the relationship to evolve naturally.

By embracing emotional availability and vulnerability, partners create an atmosphere of trust that deepens their connection. Through open sharing and empathetic listening, they establish a foundation of authenticity and mutual understanding. This, in turn, paves the way for a relationship characterized by unwavering trust and emotional intimacy.

8

Rebuilding Trust After Betrayal

Betrayals can inflict deep wounds within relationships, shaking the very foundation of trust. However, the process of rebuilding trust after breaches is not insurmountable. In this chapter, we explore the challenges inherent in restoring trust and delve into techniques that promote healing and restore security in the aftermath of betrayal.

Navigating the Challenges of Rebuilding Trust After Breaches

Rebuilding trust after a betrayal is a complex journey that demands patience, commitment, and vulnerability. It requires both partners to confront the breach and work together to mend what was broken. The challenges that arise are opportunities for growth and transformation, as they necessitate open communication, accountability, and a shared vision of healing.

Challenges of rebuilding trust:

1. Emotional Turmoil: Betrayal often triggers strong emotions such as anger, hurt, and betrayal. Partners must navigate these feelings as they work toward resolution.

2. Vulnerability: Both the betrayed and the betrayer need to embrace vulnerability to express their emotions, understand motivations, and find common ground.

3. Rebuilding Confidence: The betrayed partner may struggle to trust their judgment, while the betrayer may struggle with self-forgiveness and self-worth.

4. Restoring Security: The sense of security that was damaged needs to be rebuilt. This involves consistent actions, transparency, and reassurance.

5. Patience: Rebuilding trust takes time. Patience is required to allow healing and rebuilding to progress at a pace that feels comfortable for both partners.

Techniques for Healing and Restoring Security

1. Open Dialogue: Initiate open and honest conversations about the breach. Both partners should share their feelings, perspectives, and motivations.

2. Accountability: The betrayer must take responsibility for their actions. This involves acknowledging the breach, expressing remorse, and committing to change.

3. Empathy: The betrayer should demonstrate genuine empathy for the betrayed partner's feelings. The betrayed partner should also consider the betrayer's perspective.

4. Consistent Actions: Rebuilding trust requires consistent actions that align with words. Follow through on promises and commitments to demonstrate reliability.

5. Transparency: Be transparent about your actions, whereabouts, and intentions. Transparency rebuilds the sense of security.

6. Counseling or Therapy: Professional guidance can offer a structured approach to rebuilding trust, helping partners navigate their feelings and actions.

7. Establish Boundaries: Reestablish boundaries that promote emotional safety. Both partners should agree on what is acceptable and what is not.

8. Forgiveness: Both partners need to consider forgiveness as a part of the healing process. Forgiveness does not necessarily mean forgetting, but it can release the grip of anger.

9. Patience and Persistence: The process of rebuilding trust is not linear. There will be setbacks, but persistence and a shared commitment to growth can overcome them.

10. Shared Goals: Establish shared goals for the relationship moving forward. These goals provide a sense of purpose and direction.

11. Appreciation: Express appreciation for the effort both partners are investing in rebuilding trust. Small gestures of gratitude reinforce progress.

12. Regular Check-Ins: Periodically check in on the progress of rebuilding trust. Reflect on milestones and discuss any challenges that arise.

Rebuilding trust after a betrayal requires dedicated effort, compassion, and a willingness to confront discomfort. It's a journey that can lead to a stronger bond if both partners are committed to healing and growth. By addressing challenges openly and implementing strategies for healing, partners can create a foundation of renewed trust and security.

9

Trusting Yourself and Your Partner

Trust within a relationship isn't solely about trusting your partner; it's also about trusting yourself and your own judgment. In this chapter, we explore the significance of self-trust and its connection to trusting your partner. We also delve into strategies for cultivating self-awareness and fostering trust in your partner's intentions.

The Importance of Self-Trust within a Relationship

Self-trust is the foundation upon which your ability to trust others is built. It involves having confidence in your own judgment, values, and decisions. When you trust yourself, you're better equipped to navigate relationships with clarity and authenticity. Self-trust allows you to set healthy boundaries, communicate openly, and make decisions that align with your needs and values.

The connection between self-trust and trust in your partner:

1. Discernment: Self-trust enhances your ability to discern whether a relationship is healthy and aligned with your values.

2. Effective Communication: When you trust yourself, you're more likely to express your thoughts and emotions openly and honestly, promoting effective communication.

3. Boundaries: Self-trust enables you to set and maintain boundaries that protect your well-being within the relationship.

4. Vulnerability: Trusting yourself to handle vulnerability empowers you to be more open with your partner.

5. Conflict Resolution: Self-trust gives you the confidence to engage in conflict resolution, addressing issues constructively.

Strategies for Cultivating Self-Awareness and Trusting Your Partner's Intentions

1. Reflect on Past Experiences: Examine your past relationships and experiences to identify patterns and lessons. This reflection enhances self-awareness.

2. Practice Self-Compassion: Be kind to yourself and acknowledge that everyone makes mistakes. Self-compassion fosters self-trust.

3. Journaling: Keep a journal to record your thoughts, emotions, and reflections. This practice enhances self-awareness and clarity.

4. Mindfulness: Engage in mindfulness practices that help you stay present, attuned to your feelings, and connected to your intuition.

5. Set Clear Intentions: Clearly define your intentions for the relationship. This clarity guides your decisions and actions.

6. Communicate Needs: Communicate your needs and boundaries to your

partner openly and honestly. This fosters mutual understanding.

7. Validate Your Emotions: Trust your emotional responses and reactions. Validate your feelings and seek understanding from your partner.

8. Seek Mutual Growth: Engage in activities that promote personal growth for both you and your partner. Shared growth reinforces trust.

9. Avoid Assumptions: Instead of jumping to conclusions, seek clarification from your partner about their intentions or actions.

10. Celebrate Openness: Celebrate moments of vulnerability and honesty within the relationship. This reinforces the value of trust.

11. Express Gratitude: Express gratitude for your partner's efforts in fostering trust. Appreciation reinforces positive behaviors.

12. Reflect and Adjust: Periodically reflect on your self-trust and trust in your partner. Adjust strategies as needed to maintain a healthy balance.

Trusting yourself and your partner is a dynamic process that requires self-awareness, continuous communication, and a willingness to grow. By cultivating self-trust, you lay the foundation for a trusting relationship built on authenticity and mutual respect. Through open dialogue and shared commitment, you can navigate challenges and nurture a bond based on trust and understanding.

10

Fostering Mutual Respect and Support

Mutual respect and support are the cornerstones of a healthy and thriving relationship. In this chapter, we explore the profound impact that mutual respect has on creating a sense of security and trust. We also delve into techniques for honoring each other's boundaries and offering unwavering support, cultivating a strong foundation for trust to flourish.

How Mutual Respect Contributes to a Sense of Security

Mutual respect lays the foundation for a relationship characterized by trust and emotional safety. It involves recognizing each other's worth, values, and autonomy. When partners treat each other with respect, it creates an environment where individuality is celebrated, communication is open, and trust is nurtured. Mutual respect fosters a sense of security by assuring individuals that their feelings and boundaries will be honored.

Contributions of mutual respect:

1. Emotional Safety: Mutual respect establishes emotional safety by ensuring

CULTIVATING TRUST AND SECURITY

that both partners can express themselves without fear of ridicule or dismissal.

2. Healthy Boundaries: Respect for each other's boundaries promotes trust by demonstrating that personal limits will be acknowledged and upheld.

3. Open Communication: Partners who respect each other are more likely to engage in open and honest communication, minimizing misunderstandings.

4. Validation: Mutual respect involves validating each other's feelings and perspectives, reinforcing trust and understanding.

5. Conflict Resolution: Respectful communication during conflicts preserves the sense of security, as partners work together to find solutions.

Techniques for Honoring Each Other's Boundaries and Offering Support

1. Establish Clear Boundaries: Communicate your boundaries clearly and listen to your partner's boundaries with an open mind.

2. Respect Personal Space: Allow each other personal space and time for individual activities, fostering independence and autonomy.

3. Practice Active Listening: Pay full attention when your partner is speaking. Show respect by giving them the space to express themselves.

4. Validate Feelings: Validate your partner's emotions, even if you don't fully understand them. Show empathy and support.

5. Prioritize Equality: Treat each other as equals, valuing each other's opinions and contributions within the relationship.

6. Celebrate Differences: Embrace each other's unique qualities and perspectives. Differences can enrich the relationship.

FOSTERING MUTUAL RESPECT AND SUPPORT

7. Offer Support: Be supportive of each other's goals, aspirations, and challenges. Offer encouragement and assistance when needed.

8. Show Appreciation: Express gratitude for your partner's contributions to the relationship. Appreciation reinforces respect.

9. Communicate Intentions: Communicate your intentions and decisions openly. Transparency builds mutual trust.

10. Be Non-Judgmental: Avoid judgment or criticism when discussing sensitive topics. Create a judgment-free space for sharing.

11. Empower Decision-Making: Allow each other to make decisions and choices independently, while considering each other's input.

12. Express Commitment: Affirm your commitment to the relationship and your partner. This reaffirms your respect and support.

By fostering mutual respect and support, partners cultivate an atmosphere of trust where each person's individuality is cherished. Through open communication, validation of emotions, and a commitment to honoring boundaries, they establish a solid foundation for a relationship built on trust, security, and understanding.

11

Encouraging Personal Growth and Autonomy

Personal growth and autonomy are essential elements within a healthy relationship, contributing to individual fulfillment and a strong sense of partnership. In this chapter, we delve into the delicate balance between fostering personal development and maintaining a sense of unity. We also explore strategies for supporting each other's growth while nurturing trust and connection.

Balancing Individual Growth with a Sense of Partnership

Encouraging personal growth within a relationship involves striking a balance between individual pursuits and shared experiences. When partners are able to pursue their interests and aspirations, it enhances their sense of self and fulfillment. Simultaneously, maintaining a sense of partnership involves aligning values and goals while supporting each other's individuality. This balance creates a relationship that's characterized by mutual respect and trust.

Balancing personal growth and partnership:

ENCOURAGING PERSONAL GROWTH AND AUTONOMY

1. Mutual Support: Partners provide emotional and practical support for each other's personal growth endeavors, fostering a sense of unity.

2. Shared Values: Maintain shared values and long-term goals to ensure that personal growth doesn't compromise the partnership's foundation.

3. Autonomy: Allow each other the freedom to explore personal interests and passions, reinforcing individuality within the relationship.

4. Open Communication: Discuss personal goals and growth plans openly, keeping each other informed and aligned.

5. Quality Time: Dedicate quality time to shared experiences that reinforce the sense of partnership and deepen connections.

Strategies for Supporting Each Other's Personal Development While Maintaining Trust

1. Active Interest: Show genuine interest in your partner's personal growth endeavors. Ask questions and engage in discussions about their interests.

2. Set Goals Together: Collaboratively set short-term and long-term goals that align with each partner's individual aspirations and the relationship's direction.

3. Create Space: Respect each other's need for personal space and time to pursue individual interests and reflect on personal growth.

4. Offer Encouragement: Provide consistent encouragement and positive feedback as your partner works toward their goals.

5. Celebrate Achievements: Celebrate milestones and achievements in each other's personal growth journeys. This reinforces mutual support.

6. Balance Time Commitments: Manage time commitments to ensure that personal growth pursuits don't overshadow the relationship's needs.

7. Trust in Each Other's Intentions: Trust that your partner's pursuit of personal growth is not a threat to the relationship, but an enhancement.

8. Seek Feedback: Encourage open feedback about how each partner's personal growth efforts impact the relationship. Adjust as needed.

9. Respect Boundaries: Maintain respect for each other's boundaries. Personal growth should enhance the relationship, not strain it.

10. Check-In Regularly: Schedule regular check-ins to discuss personal goals and growth progress. Use these moments to reinforce mutual support.

11. Explore Shared Interests: Find common interests that align with both partners' personal growth goals. This fosters shared experiences.

12. Practice Gratitude: Express gratitude for the ways in which your partner's personal growth contributes positively to the relationship.

By nurturing personal growth and autonomy within the context of a partnership, individuals enhance their self-esteem and contribute to a stronger bond. Through open communication, mutual support, and a commitment to each other's well-being, partners create an environment where personal development and trust coexist harmoniously. The result is a relationship characterized by shared goals, unity, and deep respect.

12

The Ongoing Journey of Cultivating Trust and Security

Cultivating trust and security within a relationship is not a one-time task, but a continuous journey that requires dedication, effort, and mutual commitment. In this final chapter, we reflect on the perpetual nature of trust-building and the importance of nurturing an environment of ongoing growth, connection, and trust.

Reflecting on the Continuous Nature of Trust-Building and Security

Trust-building is not a destination but a dynamic process that evolves as the relationship matures. It requires consistent attention, adaptability, and a willingness to grow together. Reflecting on this ongoing nature allows partners to remain proactive, adjusting strategies as needed to ensure trust and security remain strong even as circumstances change.

Reflecting on the continuous nature:

1. Adapt to Changes: Relationships evolve over time. Be prepared to adapt

your approach to trust-building as the relationship dynamics change.

2. Learn from Challenges: Every challenge is an opportunity to learn and strengthen the foundation of trust. Approach challenges with a growth mindset.

3. Celebrate Progress: Take moments to celebrate milestones and achievements in trust-building. Recognize the progress you've made together.

4. Regular Self-Reflection: Reflect individually on your own contributions to the relationship's growth and trust. Consider what adjustments are needed.

5. Shared Reflection: Discuss trust-building and security together. Share insights, challenges, and aspirations openly.

Nurturing a Culture of Ongoing Growth, Connection, and Trust

Creating a culture of ongoing growth, connection, and trust requires consistent effort and a shared commitment. Partners who prioritize these elements lay the groundwork for a relationship that thrives through the years, deepening emotional bonds and enriching the connection.

Nurturing a culture of ongoing growth and trust:

1. Communication: Keep communication channels open and healthy. Regularly discuss goals, concerns, and progress related to trust-building.

2. Quality Time: Dedicate quality time to each other. Engage in activities that promote connection and shared experiences.

3. Continued Learning: Embrace a mindset of continuous learning about each other. This maintains the sense of discovery and curiosity.

THE ONGOING JOURNEY OF CULTIVATING TRUST AND SECURITY

4. Check-Ins: Regularly check in on each other's needs, goals, and feelings. Adjust your approach as needed to maintain alignment.

5. Prioritize Empathy: Make empathy a cornerstone of your interactions. Understand each other's perspectives and feelings.

6. Appreciation Rituals: Establish rituals that express appreciation for each other. These rituals reinforce the sense of mutual value.

7. Support Individual Growth: Continue to support each other's personal growth endeavors. Encourage each other's aspirations.

8. Conflict as Growth: Approach conflicts as opportunities for growth and understanding. Engage in constructive conflict resolution.

9. Seek New Experiences: Explore new experiences and challenges together. This fosters unity and shared memories.

10. Regular Reassessment: Periodically reassess the state of your relationship, including trust and security. Address any concerns promptly.

11. Celebrate Togetherness: Celebrate the journey you've shared and the growth you've achieved together.

12. Reaffirm Commitment: Regularly reaffirm your commitment to each other and the relationship. This verbal commitment reinforces trust.

By embracing the ongoing journey of cultivating trust and security, partners create a relationship that flourishes through mutual respect, growth, and a deep sense of connection. The journey itself becomes a source of joy and fulfillment, as partners navigate challenges, celebrate achievements, and continually strengthen the foundation of trust upon which their relationship thrives.

www.ingramcontent.com/pod-product-compliance
Lightning Source LLC
LaVergne TN
LVHW010440070526
838199LV00066B/6109